D1651826

WILD THINGS!

Monkey
in the garden

Lisa Regan

ILLUSTRATED BY **Kelly Caswell**

BLOOMSBURY

LONDON NEW DELHI NEW YORK SYDNEY

Published 2013 by
Bloomsbury Publishing Plc
50 Bedford Square, London, WC1B 3DP

www.bloomsbury.com

ISBN   HB 978-1-4081-7939-0
       PB 978-1-4081-7940-6

This book is produced using paper that is made from wood grown in managed, sustainable forests. It is natural, renewable and recyclable. The logging and manufacturing processes conform to the environmental regulations of the country of origin.

Produced for Bloomsbury Publishing by Calcium. www.calciumcreative.co.uk

Illustrated by Kelly Caswell

Picture acknowledgements: Shutterstock: Beelde Photography 23tl, ChameleonsEye 23tr.

Printed in China by Toppan Leefung

All the internet addresses given in this book were correct at the time of going to press. The author and publishers regret any inconvenience caused if addresses have changed or sites have ceased to exist, but can accept no responsibility for any such changes.

HB 10 9 8 7 6 5 4 3 2 1
PB 10 9 8 7 6 5 4 3 2 1

MIX
Paper from
responsible sources
FSC® C104723
FSC
www.fsc.org

Contents

Ring, ring. Wild thing!

If you're WILD about animals, today's your lucky day.

There's a spider monkey at the door! You could invite it in...

This guest likes to hang around!

Cool!

5

cheeky!

Monkeys are a little naughty and love to play tricks!

Sometimes, when they get upset, they even throw their poo around. Gross!

You will need

To watch out...
and clean up!

6

What a mess!

A monkey could destroy a room in minutes.

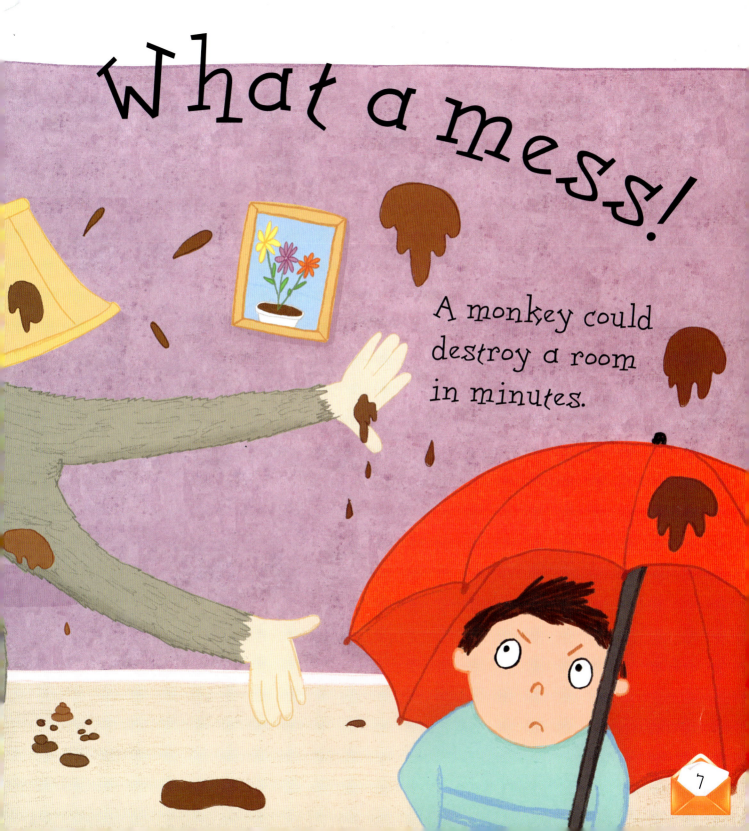

Swing on!

Monkeys move around by swinging through the trees.

Their long arms are perfect for hanging from branches.

You will need

Lots of practice on the monkey bars

Spider monkeys grip onto branches with their long fingers as they swing.

Stretch!

9

Hold on!

A monkey uses its tail like an extra arm, to grip onto branches.

Steady!

The end of a monkey's tail has a tough pad of skin.

A monkey can hang from branches by its tail alone.

You will need

To turn your home into an adventure playground

To check the ceiling when you walk into a room!

Hello, sunshine

Monkeys love warm weather.

They hide away when it is cold.

SUN CREAM

You will need

To keep the heating on all the time.

To take your monkey on sunny holidays.

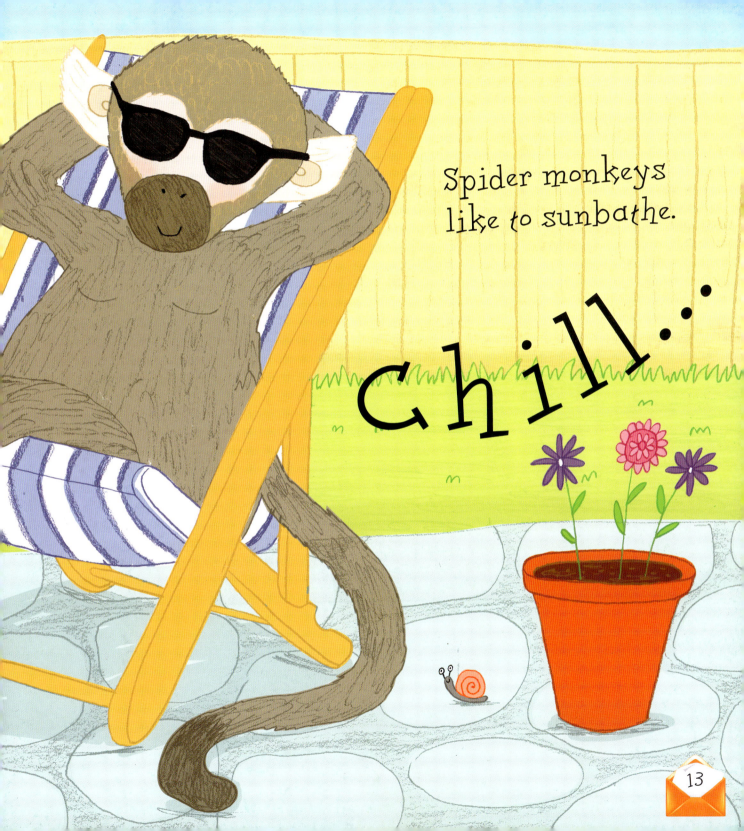

Spider monkeys
like to sunbathe.

chill...

Snack time

A spider monkey's main food is fruit.

If your monkey isn't sure what something is, it will bite it to see if it's tasty.

You will need

Daily trips to the fruit shop

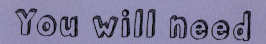

14

Yum?

Keep your favourite toys out of sight!

15

shhh!

Monkeys make a lot of noise.

They bark and scream to scare away anything that frightens them.

You will need

Ear protectors

To keep your monkey CALM!

A monkey **dictionary** to understand what your pet is saying!

Monkeys use quieter hoots and screeches to talk to their friends, too.

Screech!

17

Time to go home

Your monkey seems happy, but your parents really aren't!

18

It's time to post your pet back to its real home...

A guinea pig makes a great pet, but a spider monkey is a WILD THING!

19

Cool creatures

This book featured a spider monkey.

Spider monkeys live in Central and South America.

A mother monkey has one baby at a time. It clings to her while it is tiny.

An adult spider monkey's tail is strong enough to hold its body weight and can grow as long as 80 centimetres.

In the wild, these monkeys hardly ever come down from the treetops. They sleep high in the branches.

A tail that can be used to grip onto things is called a **prehensile tail**.

All monkeys are **primates**. This means they are **related** to **lemurs** and **apes** (including humans).

Glossary

apes very large, furry animals with powerful bodies

dictionary a book that tells you what all the words in one language mean

ear protectors pads that cover the ears to stop loud noises from hurting them

lemurs furry animals with very long tails

prehensile a tail that is used like an arm and hand for holding onto things

primate an animal group that includes apes, chimpanzees, monkeys, and humans

related when two or more things are linked to each other because they are so alike

Thanks for having me!

The Zoological Society of London (ZSL) is a charity that provides help for animals at home and worldwide. We also run ZSL London Zoo and ZSL Whipsnade Zoo.

By buying this book, you have helped us raise money to continue our work with animals around the world.

Find out more at zsl.org

ZSL
LIVING CONSERVATION

ZSL
LONDON
ZOO

ZSL
WHIPSNADE
ZOO

Take them all home!

ISBN HB 978-1-4081-7937-6
PB 978-1-4081-7938-3

ISBN HB 978-1-4081-4247-9
PB 978-1-4081-5678-0

ISBN HB 978-1-4081-4246-2
PB 978-1-4081-5679-7

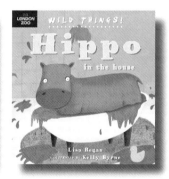

ISBN HB 978-1-4081-4245-5
PB 978-1-4081-5680-3

ISBN HB 978-1-4081-4244-8
PB 978-1-4081-5681-0

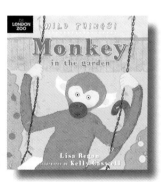

ISBN HB 978-1-4081-7939-0
PB 978-1-4081-7940-6

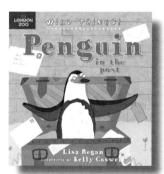

ISBN HB 978-1-4081-7941-3
PB 978-1-4081-7942-0

ISBN HB 978-1-4081-7935-2
PB 978-1-4081-7936-9